RUNNING DRY

THE GLOBAL WATER CRISIS

STUART A. KALLEN

TWENTY-FIRST CENTURY BOOKS / MINNEAPOLIS

This book is dedicated to the scientists, researchers, activists, and engaged citizens working to bring water issues to light and to ensure that our children's children's children will have fresh sparkling water.

Twenty-First Century Books
A division of Lerner Publishing Group, Inc.
241 First Avenue North
Minneapolis, MN 55401 USA

For reading levels and more information, look up this title at www.lernerbooks.com.

Main body text set in Janson Text LT Std 11/15.
Typeface provided by Adobe Systems.

Library of Congress Cataloging-in-Publication Data

Kallen, Stuart A., 1955–
    Running dry : the global water crisis / by Stuart A. Kallen.
        pages   cm
    Includes bibliographical references and index.
    ISBN 978–1–4677–2646–7 (lib. bdg. : alk. paper)
    ISBN 978–1–4677–6308–0 (eBook)
    1. Water-supply—Juvenile literature. 2. Water consumption—Juvenile literature.
  3. Water conservation—Juvenile literature. 4. Water—Pollution—Juvenile literature.
  I. Title.
    TD348.K36 2015
    333.91'16—dc23   2014003223

Manufactured in the United States of America
1 – DP – 12/31/14

CONTENTS

INTRODUCTION
Water for Life   **4**

CHAPTER 1
Tainted Water   **8**

CHAPTER 2
A Hungry and Thirsty World   **20**

CHAPTER 3
Supply and Demand   **30**

CHAPTER 4
Water in a Changing Climate   **42**

SOURCE NOTES   55
GLOSSARY   57
SELECTED BIBLIOGRAPHY   58
FURTHER INFORMATION   60
INDEX   62

Freshwater found in rivers, lakes, aquifers, and glaciers is critical to life on Earth. Plants and animals cannot live without clean freshwater, but supplies are under attack from pollution, drought, and overuse.

Introduction

WATER FOR LIFE

Water is the basis of all life on Earth. It is necessary for survival. The average person can live only about three days without drinking water. Water makes up about two-thirds of the body of every living creature, including humans. It is so abundant on Earth that Robert Kandel, a scientist with the National Aeronautics and Space Administration (NASA), has commented that "some would have us call our planet not 'Earth' but 'Ocean' in honor of the liquid vastness that covers over two-thirds of the globe."

In 2012 NASA published a spectacular photograph of Earth taken by a satellite flying 435 miles (700 kilometers) above the planet. In the photograph, known as *Blue Marble 2012*, Earth resembles a toy marble. The picture shows swirling white clouds encircling the deep blue waters of Earth. In looking at the image, two things are immediately obvious: the blue planet hangs in the black emptiness of space, and most of Earth is covered in water.

FRESH AND SALTY

About 98 percent of Earth's water is seawater, which is 3.5 percent salt. Although humans need a small amount of salt to survive, seawater has too much for people to drink. Were someone to drink a few glasses of seawater, the high salt content would create a chemical imbalance in the body, resulting in massive dehydration and the risk of death. Salt water is also deadly to most land animals and plants and can't be used to water crops.

Only about 2 percent of water on Earth is freshwater (water without salt). But most of Earth's freshwater is frozen, locked up in ice caps and glaciers. Liquid water available for drinking—the water in lakes, rivers, streams, and underground deposits called aquifers—makes up less than 0.5 percent of all the water on the planet. If all the water on Earth could fit in a 1-gallon (3.8-liter) bucket, only 1 tablespoon (15 milliliters) would be liquid freshwater.

Most freshwater is not used for drinking. About 70 percent of the available freshwater on Earth is used to grow food, which feeds Earth's 7.2 billion-plus people. At least 20 percent of Earth's freshwater is used for industrial purposes. Only 10 percent of freshwater goes for household purposes, such as drinking, bathing, flushing toilets, washing clothes and cars, and watering lawns.

UNDER ASSAULT

According to the US Census Bureau, the world's human population increases by about 80 million people annually. This is equivalent to adding ten times the population of New York City to Earth every year. The exploding population requires more food, water, and manufactured goods. For example, newly industrialized nations such as China, India, and Kenya will need about 50 percent more water by the year 2025 to supply their growing manufacturing sectors. Already industrialized countries, such as France, Great Britain, and the United States, will need about 18 percent more water by 2025.

But even as demand for water grows, supplies do not. In fact, Earth's freshwater resources are being depleted and contaminated at alarming rates. Some of the depletion comes from overuse. For instance, in the midwestern United States, people pull more than 1.5 billion gallons (5.7 billion liters) of water from the Ogallala Aquifer

The city of Guiyu, China, is home to thousands of small workshops that process e-waste, or electronic waste. Workers there break down old computers, cell phones, and other electronic devices to salvage the gold, copper, lead, and other metals inside them. Waste from the workshops has polluted the river that runs through Guiyu.

each day for agriculture, industry, and household use. As a result, the average water level in the aquifer has fallen by about two-thirds. Much water is also lost to waste. Every day in the United States, 7 billion gallons (26.5 billion liters) of clean drinking water go down the drain from leaking household faucets. This is enough to fill more than eleven thousand swimming pools every twenty-four hours.

Pollution is another major problem. Across the globe, freshwater is tainted by a wide variety of polluting materials, including paints, pesticides, petroleum, plastics, and heavy metals such as lead and copper. In addition, in poor nations such as India, Afghanistan, Pakistan, and many countries in Africa, millions of citizens do not have access to toilets. They often relieve themselves directly into rivers, lakes, and streams, polluting these waterways with raw sewage. The waste can carry bacteria and parasites, causing illnesses such as diarrhea, dysentery, and cholera in people who drink from sewage-infested waterways. Every twenty-one seconds, somewhere in a poor nation, a child dies from drinking filthy water.

Burning fossil fuels such as gasoline (which comes from crude oil), coal, and natural gas also threatens freshwater supplies. When fossil fuels burn, they release carbon dioxide and other greenhouse gases into the atmosphere. Greenhouse gases trap the sun's heat in the same way the glass roof of a greenhouse traps solar heat. As humans continue to burn more fossil fuels every year, more greenhouse gases lead to more trapped heat and to global warming, or higher temperatures on Earth. Most scientists agree that these trends are creating climate change. Shifts in Earth's climate in turn create weather extremes such as drought, flooding, and massive storms.

Extended droughts caused by global warming are drying up rivers, lakes, and aquifers across the globe. In parts of Africa, for instance, crops and livestock in drought-affected regions have died for lack of water, causing an estimated 2 million human deaths from starvation.

The fight over water rights has increased tensions between nations. In northern Africa, for example, Egypt and the Sudan are struggling over control of the Nile River. Turkey, Iraq, and other nations in the Middle East dispute rights to freshwater from the Tigris and Euphrates Rivers. Between 2006 and 2010, severe drought in the Middle Eastern nation of Syria caused around 1.5 million people to abandon their farms, animal herds, and ranches. The refugees flooded into cities, but the Syrian government did little to provide them with jobs, schooling, health care, or food. The situation, along with internal political and economic pressures, resulted in widespread protests, which erupted into civil war in 2011.

Water is a basic human necessity and a commodity that drives the world economy. Factories use massive amounts of water to produce cell phones, soda pop, and cars. Energy companies use vast amounts of water to extract fossil fuels from Earth. Private businesses have increasingly moved to buy the rights to freshwater supplies, in many cases depriving local communities of much-needed water. The availability and control of freshwater supplies are issues poised to define life in the twenty-first century.

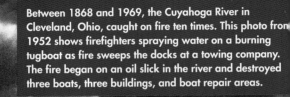

Chapter 1

TAINTED WATER

Spanning more than 750 miles (1,207 km) from east to west, the Great Lakes Basin is the largest freshwater system on Earth's surface. The Great Lakes (Superior, Michigan, Huron, Erie, and Ontario) straddle the border between the United States and Canada and are fed by major waterways including the Chicago, Detroit, Niagara, Cuyahoga, and Saint Lawrence Rivers. Together the Great Lakes and their rivers contain 21 percent of the world's freshwater supply and 84 percent of all freshwater in North America. For much of the twentieth century, however, the Great Lakes Basin also contained the most polluted waters in the world.

Like the banks of many other major rivers feeding the Great Lakes, those of the Cuyahoga—which flows through Cleveland, Ohio, and into Lake Erie—were once lined with oil refineries, paint factories, chemical plants, and steel foundries. For many years, these industries dumped oily residue and chemical waste into the river. On June 22, 1969, sparks—possibly from the wheels of a passing freight train—caused oil, residue, and chemicals in the Cuyahoga to burst into flames. It was the tenth fire on the river since 1868 and the first to make national headlines. A cover story in *Time* magazine described the state of the water before the fire:

Some River! Chocolate-brown, oily, bubbling with subsurface gases, it oozes rather than flows. "Anyone who falls into the Cuyahoga does not drown," Cleveland's citizens joke grimly. "He decays." . . . The lower Cuyahoga has no visible signs of life, not even low forms such as leeches and sludge worms that usually thrive on wastes.

COMING CLEAN

Firefighters put out the fire in about twenty-five minutes, but the burning Cuyahoga River led to national outrage and to international embarrassment. In response to this and to other environmental disasters of the era, the US Congress established the Environmental Protection Agency (EPA) in 1970. The federal agency was tasked with setting, monitoring, and enforcing regulations to protect human health, wildlife, land, water, and air.

With the creation of the EPA, Congress then passed several laws to protect US waters. At the time, only one-third of US lakes and rivers were free of sewage, oil, pesticides, and heavy metals. Some cities dumped raw sewage directly into big rivers, including the Hudson and the Mississippi. Few legal limits on waste discharges from factories were in place to protect waterways. As a result, fish populations were dying, and many beaches were unsafe for swimming.

The Clean Water Act (CWA), enacted in 1972, required the EPA to identify and prevent point source pollution. This is pollution discharged from a single source, such as an oil refinery, paint factory, or sewage treatment plant. The law required factories and wastewater treatment plants to use pollution-control devices to drastically limit or eliminate pollution discharges into waterways. In addition, the CWA provided money for cities to construct nearly five thousand sewer systems and three thousand water treatment plants.

SHUTTING OFF THE TAPS IN CHARLESTON

Countless chemical storage tanks sit along rivers and other waterways throughout the United States. Some of these huge cylindrical tanks hold tens of thousands of gallons of deadly chemicals, yet they are largely unregulated and rarely inspected. Most Americans were unaware of this until January 9, 2014, when the chemical 4-methylcyclohexanemethanol (MCHM) leaked from a storage tank and contaminated the drinking water supply of three hundred thousand people in Charleston, West Virginia.

MCHM is a cleaner used to process coal, an abundant energy resource in West Virginia. About 10,000 gallons (37,854 liters) of MCHM leaked from a small hole in the bottom of a stainless-steel tank on Charleston's Elk River. Owned by a company called Freedom Industries, the tank had last been inspected by government officials in 1991. The Elk River drains into the Kanawha River about 1 mile (1.6 km) upstream from Charleston's drinking water treatment plant. The contaminated water was sucked from the river into the plant's main intake pipe.

The chemical leak was discovered after local residents described a sweet, liquorish-like smell coming from their tap water. Within hours, officials shut down Charleston's only drinking water supply. West Virginians in nine counties surrounding the Charleston metropolitan area were warned not to use their water for drinking, cooking, bathing, or cleaning. People rushed out to buy bottled water from stores.

Although coal producers have used MCHM for decades, few studies have examined the chemical's long-term effect on human health and wildlife populations. The substance in the water caused hundreds of Charleston citizens to suffer short-term reactions such as nausea, vomiting, dizziness, headaches, and diarrhea. Many West Virginians are worried about what may happen to their health in the future.

Charleston residents line up at a parking lot to receive free bottled water a few days after a chemical spill contaminated their city's drinking water supply.

Nine days later, on January 18, authorities declared that the city water was once again safe to drink, but the incident left many people doubting the safety of the city's water supply. Many continue to drink bottled water. Meanwhile, Freedom Industries declared bankruptcy, which means the company won't have to pay compensation to West Virginians harmed by the water contamination.

In 1974 Congress passed the Safe Drinking Water Act (SDWA) to further protect public health by ensuring the safety of US tap water. When the act went into effect, more than one-third of all tap water in the United States contained unsafe levels of hazardous chemicals. The SDWA required public water systems to test for and drastically reduce levels of industrial toxins, chemicals, heavy metals, and bacteria in drinking water. Amendments to the act required water companies to publish annual consumer confidence reports. The reports identify pollutants in drinking water and explain their possible health impacts.

In 2012, when the Clean Water Act celebrated its fortieth anniversary, experts agreed that the law had been revolutionary. Pollution-control devices, testing, and sewage treatment plants have dramatically cleaned up US waterways. In addition, because of a changing economy, many of the manufacturing plants that once lined US rivers and lakes have closed their doors. Cities such as Cleveland, Ohio; Detroit, Michigan; and Pittsburgh, Pennsylvania, no longer have giant factories discharging waste into waterways. Although US waters are still polluted, experts say they are cleaner than they were in the 1960s. Wisconsin Wildlife Federation president Chuck Matyska explained, "Before passage of the Clean Water Act, people treated waterways like open sewers. Now . . . fish populations are back. . . . [T]he Clean Water Act is a winner for people and wildlife."

ANIMAL FARMS

Even with improvements in water quality and water safety, freshwater in the United States still faces major, ongoing threats. For instance, the Clean Water Act does little to address nonpoint source pollution, or widely dispersed contamination from numerous sources. Nonpoint source pollution includes motor oil, gasoline, antifreeze, and other toxic chemicals that leak from cars and trucks; fertilizers, herbicides, and pesticides from farms; and chemicals that leak from mining operations, abandoned factories, and gas stations. These pollutants seep into aquifers and wash into rivers, lakes, and streams when it rains or snows. While various federal, state, and local laws have been passed to regulate nonpoint source pollution, it remains a significant problem. The pollution comes from so many sources that control measures are extremely difficult and expensive to implement.

The Clean Water Act also does not address pollution from large-scale farming facilities called concentrated animal feeding operations (CAFOs). In the United States, a growing percentage of animals killed for food are raised at CAFOs. In 2013 these "factory farms" produced more than half of the 1 billion US animals slaughtered for food annually.

The basin of the Cape Fear River in North Carolina has more CAFOs than anywhere else on Earth. The basin covers more than 16 percent of the state and contains more than 6,200 miles (10,000 km) of streams and rivers. CAFOs in the Cape Fear Basin process more than 5 million hogs, 16 million turkeys, and 300 million chickens annually. A single CAFO with 80,000 hogs creates more than 15 million tons (13.6 million metric tons) of waste every year. This is 1.5 times the sewage created by all residents in the city of Philadelphia, Pennsylvania, each year.

EPA regulations put in place in the 1970s require towns and cities to clean wastewater at sewage treatment plants. These facilities filter solid wastes from sewage, add chemicals to the remaining water to kill germs, and then release the water back into lakes and rivers. Laws do not regulate CAFO wastes in the same way, however. Instead, CAFOs are allowed to store animal manure in large outdoor lagoons, which can hold tens of millions of gallons of liquid waste. The waste contains a range of harmful pollutants. For instance, often CAFOs spray chemical insecticides onto live animals for pest control. Trace amounts of the chemicals make their way into the animals' bodies, and they are later excreted in manure. CAFO operations sometimes also feed animals nutritional supplements containing heavy metals such as zinc and copper. These metals too are excreted in animal manure. Additionally, the waste can contain deadly viruses and bacteria, such as salmonella.

Some lagoons include heavy composite liners to prevent seepage, but even with liners, all animal waste lagoons leak to some degree. Some lagoons flood during hurricanes and other storms. Occasionally, lagoons break and spill their contents into waterways. In 1995, for example, a lagoon in Onslow County ruptured and spilled 22 million gallons (83.3 million liters) of manure into North Carolina's New River. The spill killed 10 million fish and countless other aquatic creatures. When Hurricane Floyd hit North Carolina four years later, at least five manure lagoons burst, while another forty-seven overflowed, sending toxic waste into rivers. In 2012 the EPA reported that waste generated by large-scale hog, chicken, and cattle operations had polluted more than 35,000 miles (56,327 km) of rivers and contaminated groundwater in seventeen US states.

Environmentalists think the CWA should be expanded to address pollution from factory farms, but big business is pushing back. Many industries oppose existing EPA regulations and fight hard to keep them from expanding further. For instance, the factory farm industry argues that expanded water pollution regulations would increase business costs. These costs would have to be passed onto consumers in the form of higher meat prices, industry leaders say. Factory farming is a multibillion-dollar industry, and it uses its financial strength to lobby against new environmental regulations it views as harmful to business.

While CAFOs originated in the United States, they are becoming numerous in poorer nations, including China, Bangladesh, India, and many countries in eastern Europe and in Africa. These nations have weak environmental laws, and most animal waste from CAFOs there is dumped into rivers, lakes, and streams.

FRACK ATTACK

As the world becomes more industrialized, with more factories and with more people driving cars every year, demand for energy is greater than ever before. To meet this demand, energy companies have devised new technologies for extracting fossil fuels from underground deposits. One example is hydraulic fracturing, commonly called fracking, to extract natural gas and oil trapped in deep underground shale formations. Fracking is big business in states with large shale formations, including Texas, Colorado, and Pennsylvania.

Fracking involves constructing a wellbore—a steel-encased well—from the surface to the gas or oil far below. Drillers then blast a mixture of water, sand, and hundreds of toxic chemicals into the wellbore under extremely high pressure. Over the course of three to ten days, the liquid fractures the shale, freeing the gas or oil trapped between the layers. Workers then pump the gas or oil and the fracking water up through the wellbore to storage tanks at the surface.

Fracking uses vast amounts of water—between 2 to 10 million gallons (7.6 to 37.9 million liters) of water for a single well. To obtain a steady supply of water for fracking, energy companies purchase the rights to pump water from streams, lakes, and aquifers from the local government water boards that control supplies. The massive use of water for fracking has drained rivers, lakes, and aquifers in some places. In addition, fracking produces huge amounts of wastewater that contains dissolved chemicals and other forms of toxic pollution.

Fracking operations often send wastewater to water treatment plants, but most of these facilities are not equipped to remove salt and chemical toxins from water. In 2011 the *New York Times* conducted a study of fracking fluid disposal at water treatment plants in Pennsylvania. The *Times* found that high levels of salt in the liquid caused metal pipes and other equipment to rust and corrode at alarming levels.

Tests revealed that the Pennsylvania fracking fluids also contained high levels of radium and uranium, radioactive substances from soil that mixed with fracking water deep underground. These substances, which are known to cause cancer, cannot be removed by standard water treatment techniques and thus remain in water supplies and also leak into wells. Some places in Pennsylvania have measured radium and uranium in drinking water at levels thousands of times higher than those allowed by the Safe Drinking Water Act.

FRACTIVISTS FIGHT FRACKING

Hydraulic fracturing has created a new type of protester called a fractivist. In taking on gas drilling companies, fractivists are fighting one of the wealthiest and most influential industries in the world. The heart of the anti-fracking movement is in northern Pennsylvania, where hydraulic fracturing has drastically increased since the first decade of the 2000s.

Two citizens in the region, Sue Rapp and Vera Scroggins, are leaders of the fractivist movement. Because state and federal laws do not regulate fracking, Rapp and Scroggins have worked to enact fracking bans in more than one hundred Pennsylvania communities, including towns and counties. The big city of Pittsburgh, Pennsylvania, has also enacted a fracking ban. The two women have spoken with congressional representatives, organized protests, and enlisted movie stars such as Matt Damon, Robert De Niro, and Susan Sarandon to speak out against fracking.

Still the process goes on. In 2014 Pennsylvania's Susquehanna County had seven hundred gas wells, and gas companies had identified another three thousand possible drilling locations in the area. One reason that fracking continues, despite the dangers and opposition, is that many powerful politicians support the gas industry. The industry brings jobs and other economic benefits to local communities, many of which are poor, and also contributes generously to the campaigns of pro-fracking politicians.

Gas drilling companies are not legally required to reveal the chemical makeup of the fracking fluids they use. But scientists know that fracking fluids contain about 630 chemicals, including hydrochloric acid, kerosene, diesel fuel, and toluene. These deadly substances are linked to cancer and other ailments. According to a 2010 study by environmental health analyst Theo Colborn, 93 percent of these fracking chemicals are known to sicken people and animals. Forty-three percent of the chemicals are classified as endocrine disruptors, which have been linked to childhood and adult cancers, infertility, attention deficit hyperactivity disorder, autism, diabetes, and thyroid disorders.

Fracking frequently takes place near homes and farms—anywhere energy companies have purchased the right to drill from landowners. In many areas where fracking is widespread, people get their drinking water from wells drilled into aquifers. Sometimes fracking fluids spill from tanks or leak from wellbores, and over time, chemicals in the fluids migrate to aquifers through fissures in the rock, contaminating

Sherry Vargson of Granville Summit, Pennsylvania, allowed an energy company to drill for natural gas on her farm. Methane from drilling operations leached into her well water. When she holds a flame to her kitchen faucet, methane causes the running water to ignite.

homeowners' well water. People with contaminated wells must buy bottled water—a pricey alternative—for drinking, bathing, and cooking. Some people have sued energy companies over water contamination caused by fracking operations.

Additionally, flammable methane, which is the main ingredient in natural gas, has also migrated from fracking operations to water wells in Pennsylvania, Colorado, and elsewhere. Tap water containing methane can be ignited with the touch of a lit match. Some Americans have abandoned their homes because the methane-polluted water is undrinkable and the risk of a massive explosion is too great.

Despite the physical evidence, gas and oil industry officials have long denied that fracking pollutes groundwater. Whatever the case, fracking is largely exempt from environmental protection laws. The Safe Drinking Water Act previously defined "pollution" as solid waste, sewage, garbage, chemical waste, and other related substances. In 2005 the oil and gas industry pressured Congress to amend the law to change the definition of "pollution." The new law reads, "This term [*pollution*] does not mean . . . water, gas, or other material which is injected into a well to facilitate production of oil or gas." The change in wording is known as the Halliburton Loophole. It was written into law at the urging of then US vice president Dick Cheney, former head of Halliburton Company, which earns billions of dollars annually producing fracking fluids and oil drilling equipment.

Like CAFOs, hydraulic fracturing is spreading from the United States to other nations around the world. In 2013 India, Russia, Argentina, and China all expanded the fracking of their shale formations.

GOING VIRAL IN CHINA

Water pollution is an acute problem in China. The country lacks environmental protection laws such as the Clean Water Act, and many Chinese rivers are as polluted as the Cuyahoga was in the 1960s. In fact, in 2013 China's minister of environmental protection noted that at least one-quarter of the country's rivers were too contaminated for drinking, watering crops, and even for industrial use. Yet with no alternative options, farmers have no choice but to use this foul water on their crops, and people rely on it for drinking. As Bulgarian-born environmental journalist Nadya Ivanova explains, "Much of China's water is so contaminated that it should not even be touched, yet tremendous amounts of the grains, vegetables, and fruits that are served in homes and restaurants, as well as [crops such as cotton that are made into] textiles that are sold in markets, are irrigated with untreated industrial wastewater."

As in the United States and many other parts of the world, efforts to prevent water pollution in China pit protesters and environmental groups against private industry and government officials. Protesting is restricted in China by law, and those who speak out against government or industry can lose their jobs and homes and face imprisonment. Despite the risks, Chinese activists have taken to social media to publicize pollution concerns and to shame the government into action.

Jin Zengmin is one of the most renowned Chinese activists. In January 2013, Jin made an offer to Bao Zhenmin, the chief of a local government environmental agency in Zhejiang Province. Jin offered to pay Bao the equivalent of $32,000 to swim in a polluted local river for twenty minutes. Jin announced his offer on Sina Weibo, the Twitter-like social media service in China. Bao did not take Jin up on his offer.

The banks of the polluted river are lined by more than one hundred shoe factories. According to Jin, who was born in the 1960s, "When I was a child, people swam or washed vegetables in the river. But those factories use chemical raw materials to make shoes and dump their industrial waste directly into the river." Jin blamed the early death of his sister on the pollution. She was stricken with cancer at the age of thirty-five.

Jin's antipollution campaign went viral on the Internet: millions of people viewed the post and passed it along to others. Within days,

Two factories that were operating illegally dumped toxic chemicals into the Jianhe River in Luoyang, China. The local government shut the factories down, but many factories in China continue to dump industrial waste into waterways.

thousands of Chinese citizens had posted pictures on Sina Weibo of polluted rivers where they lived. According to Chinese water expert Ma Jun, "The appeals made by Jin Zengmin and other Weibo users force people to face up to water pollution and have attracted more people to join the antipollution campaign. [Internet activism] can prevent local governments from standing in line with the heavy polluters."

A QUESTION OF BALANCE

At the time of the Sina Weibo campaign, polls in China showed that 41 percent of people believed water pollution was a very big problem. In 2011 a poll commissioned by the Civil Society Institute in the United States showed that 91 percent of Americans wanted Congress to protect US waterways.

Regulating industries to prevent polluting practices can be expensive and time-consuming. But plants, animals, and humans cannot live without clean freshwater. Are the material needs of society, from inexpensive shoes to animal-based foods and carbon-based energy sources, so critical that freshwater bodies can be sacrificed?

Chapter 2

A HUNGRY AND THIRSTY WORLD

A farmer on Gold Island in Cairo, Egypt, tends an irrigation channel that brings water from the Nile River to agricultural fields. People have used canal irrigation since the earliest days of farming.

More than five thousand years ago, ancient Egyptians constructed a complex system of dams and canals along the Nile River. When the river flooded as a result of seasonal rains each year, its waters traveled through this irrigation system onto farm fields. When the floodwaters receded, farmers used the moist, nutrient-rich black soil to raise wheat, barley, and other crops. The Nile irrigation system allowed the ancient Egyptians to prosper and thrive in the harsh desert climate of northern Africa.

For thousands of years, civilizations in arid regions used canal irrigation systems similar to those of the Egyptians. The ancient Chinese, Persians, Romans, and American Indians all used canal irrigation. Traditional canal irrigation methods are still utilized by farmers worldwide, even in the twenty-first century.

PUMPING WATER

For centuries, farmers augmented canal irrigation systems with windmills, which powered pumps that brought groundwater up to the surface. In the nineteenth century, windmills opened up arid regions of the Great Plains, from Texas to North Dakota, to small-scale farming and ranching. A farmer could irrigate around 15 acres (6 hectares) with the water pumped by a single windmill. This method of irrigation supplemented canals fed with water from the Platte, Arkansas, and other rivers of the Great Plains.

In the United States, in the early 1950s, most farmers replaced windmills with diesel- and electric-powered pumps that tapped into aquifers. Unlike windmills, modern pumps can bring thousands of gallons of groundwater to the surface every minute, allowing farmers to irrigate huge expanses of land.

Most modern farmers use devices called center-pivot irrigators. These irrigation machines on wheels are designed to pivot, or turn, around a wellbore. A center-pivot irrigator can water a circle of land about 1 mile (1.6 km) in diameter. The irrigators allow farmers to produce large harvests on land that was once too dry for farming. In 2014 an average acre (0.4 hectares) of irrigated land in Kansas produced twice as many bushels of corn, two-thirds more soybeans, and three-fifths more wheat than land watered by rainfall alone.

THE OGALLALA AQUIFER

Many farmers in Kansas pump water from the Ogallala Aquifer. This vast underground source of freshwater formed around four million years ago. The Ogallala covers more than 170,000 square miles (440,297 sq. km) beneath all or part of eight arid states: South Dakota, Wyoming, Colorado, Nebraska, Kansas, Oklahoma, Texas, and New Mexico. The Ogallala is one of the world's most important aquifers. It provides about one-third of all water used for irrigation in the United States while supplying drinking water to millions of people.

But by the late twentieth century, farmers were emptying the aquifer faster than rainwater could replenish it. When center-pivot irrigators were first developed in the 1950s, the average water depth in the Ogallala Aquifer was 240 feet (73 meters). While only a few thousand farmers installed center-pivot systems during the 1950s, the irrigators grew increasingly popular. By 1980 more than 170,000

A center-pivot irrigation system waters alfalfa crops on the US Great Plains. The irrigator pumps water from the Ogallala Aquifer beneath the plains. But water levels in the aquifer are dropping quickly.

wells were sucking groundwater from the Ogallala Aquifer, and water levels were falling as much as 6 feet (2 m) per year in some places. Rainfall was replenishing the water at a rate of only 0.5 inches (13 millimeters) per year and in some areas even less.

By 2014 massive water withdrawals had reduced the average depth of the aquifer by two-thirds, to about 80 feet (24 m). In Kansas at least one-quarter of the wells in the state were running dry. Scientists predict that if the rates of depletion continue, the Ogallala will run completely dry by 2040.

DRY WELLS

Like the Ogallala, aquifers throughout the world are running dry. In 2014 eighteen countries, home to half the world's people, were overpumping their aquifers. This overpumping is expected to have a negative impact on global grain harvests, according to Lester R. Brown, president of the Earth Policy Institute of Washington, DC. He writes, "The question is not whether water shortages will affect future harvests in these countries, but rather when they will do so."

The overpumping problem is most acute in India, the world's number three grain producer. India has about 16 percent of the world's population but only 4 percent of its water. The nation has no restrictions on water well drilling, and Indian farmers have drilled 27 million wells since the mid-1990s. In 2014 around 53 percent of the food grown in India was irrigated with groundwater.

The use of groundwater for irrigation has resulted in much larger grain harvests—but at a cost. In the northern part of the Indian state of Gujarat, for example, underground water levels are falling by 20 feet (6 m) per year. In the southern Indian state of Tamil Nadu, 95 percent of wells used by small-acreage farmers have dried up.

With overuse of this proportion, water sources dry up, crops don't grow, and food shortages become widespread. According to a survey sponsored by Save the Children, a charity organization, one out of four people in India experiences an occasional foodless day, when they do not eat at all. In 2010 the *Times of India* reported that half of all childhood deaths in India result from malnutrition, or poor diet. That number is expected to grow as the nation's population increases, placing increasing strain on limited water sources and on related food supplies.

HARVESTING THE MONSOON

Although India has groundwater shortages, the nation receives a lot of rain—on average, 46 inches (117 centimeters) of rain each year. However, India's rain is a result of a seasonal rain pattern called a monsoon. In late spring, India is dry and sweltering until the monsoons begin in June. The rains continue until September. A monsoon is formed as heat rises into the sky and pulls in cool, moist air from an ocean. In India the collision of warm air with the cold air from the Indian Ocean causes sheets of rain to gush down on the landscape, flooding villages, farms, and forests. Some years, however, the monsoon rains don't come. Then the nation faces catastrophic drought and starvation.

The use of a simple, ancient technique called pond digging is lessening the disastrous impact of the boom-and-bust monsoon cycle in India. Rajendra Singh, an Indian water activist and conservationist, has actively promoted this method of saving water. Singh has a background in medicine. In the 1980s, he moved to the remote dry hills of the state of Rajasthan in northwestern India to work as a village doctor. But he soon learned that farmers in Rajasthan were more worried about water than about their health. Singh decided to build a pond to catch rainwater during the short but intense monsoon season. Over the next four years, Singh dug out an area covering 3.5 acres (1.4 hectares), sometimes working twelve hours a day. When it rained, the pond filled with water, which farmers and their families then used for drinking and to irrigate crops. The water-filled pond had an unexpected benefit on the surrounding environment. Some of the water from the pond seeped underground naturally, recharging the local aquifer and greening about 500 acres (202 hectares) nearby.

People came from miles around to admire Singh's work. Impressed with what they saw, they went back to their villages and

In places with seasonal rains, people can capture water during the rainy season for use in the dry season. This water catchment pond is on a coffee plantation in Kenya.

created their own rainwater harvesting ponds. According to Singh, "The wonderful thing is . . . more than 30 villages start the work. The next year, it's 200 villages. . . . This work [is] made by community effort! No grant from the government. No grant from the World Bank or UN [United Nations, an international peacekeeping and humanitarian organization]. Nothing!"

By 2013 people had constructed more than ten thousand rainwater harvesting structures in twelve hundred Indian villages. The pools not only provide water for drinking and agriculture but also overflow from the ponds to seven major rivers that were once dry most of the year.

Singh has become a well-known figure internationally. In addition to pond digging, he has worked to stop the construction of breweries, mines, and other facilities in India that consume massive amounts of water. He has also introduced farmers to crops that need less water. According to Singh, "Water conservation and community-driven, decentralized water management is the solution for my country. . . . If we look at the gap between supply and demand in 2050, 80 percent of that gap can be closed purely by these improvements—which are going to increase water efficiency on the farms, without doing anything else."

Like India, the United States is focusing on improving efficiency in the use of water. In parts of the southern United States, for example, an extreme drought between 2010 and 2013 pushed farmers to switch from water-guzzling wheat and corn crops to sorghum, which requires significantly less water to grow.

US farmers are also switching from center-pivot irrigation to drip irrigation systems, also known as trickle- or micro-irrigation systems. Rather than spraying crops from above, these irrigators sit on the ground, allowing water to drip slowly onto plants. By delivering water directly to the base of plants, drip irrigators lose less water to evaporation and can cut agricultural water use by as much as 70 percent.

BIOFUEL FROM CORN

Corn makes up 90 percent of all the crops that are fed by water from the Ogallala Aquifer. Thirty percent of this corn is used as an ingredient in human food and beverages. Another 30 percent is used to feed livestock and poultry. Forty percent of the corn is turned into an alcohol-based biofuel called ethanol, which is mixed with gasoline and used to power motor vehicles.

A 2005 mandate by the EPA requires gasoline to contain 10 percent ethanol. Supporters of the ethanol program maintain that using the biofuel makes the United States less dependent on foreign oil imports. In addition, when burned, ethanol produces less carbon dioxide, a key climate-change gas, than petroleum-based gasoline does.

But critics of the ethanol policy point out flaws with the mandate. Ethanol raises the price of fuel because it is more expensive than gasoline to produce, transport, and handle. And using ethanol doesn't provide much reduction in overall carbon dioxide production because farmers use tractors and other vehicles, which run on vast amounts of diesel fuel, to grow and harvest corn before turning the crop into ethanol. So do the trucks that transport the fuel. In addition, the growth of the biofuel industry has driven up the price of corn, making corn-based foods more expensive.

The corn for ethanol production also relies on nitrogen-based fertilizers, which run off into major river systems such as the Mississippi in the Midwest. The fertilizer residue leads to explosive growth of algae, which then die and sink to the bottom of the waterway, where bacteria feed on the organic matter. The bacteria depletes the water of critical oxygen, leading to so-called dead zones where marine life can no longer survive. The Gulf of Mexico, for example, at the mouth of the Mississippi River, has the largest dead zone in the United States, much of it related to fertilizer-based pollution.

Ethanol production is also very water intensive: it takes 800 gallons (3,028 liters) of water to produce just 1 gallon (3.7 liters) of ethanol. Biofuel production accounts for only 1 percent of the total water withdrawal from the Ogallala Aquifer. But according to a report by the Environmental Defense Fund, "It is an incremental withdrawal from an already unsustainable resource. . . . It is equivalent to 'mining' the water resource, and the loss of the resource is essentially irreversible."

WHERE'S THE BEEF?

Raising plant crops consumes vast amounts of water, but raising cattle, the source of beef, uses even more. About 65 percent of a cow's body weight is water, and fresh drinking water is essential to the animal's health. Water is also critical for growing the grain that cattle eat to survive. Growing the feed to produce just 1 pound (0.45 kilograms) of beef requires approximately 2,500 gallons (9,464 liters) of water, and Americans eat about 53 billion pounds (24 billion kg) of beef every year.

With predictions of significant water shortages in coming decades, some ecologists favor a global shift to a vegetarian diet as a smart way to conserve water. In contrast to beef, producing 1 pound (0.45 kg) of rice or tofu (a soybean product) requires just 228 gallons (863 liters) of water. Worldwide, humans derive about 20 percent of their protein from animal-based foods (meat, eggs, and dairy products). By the year 2050, water resources may no longer be sufficient to support the production of current levels of animal-based foods, and people may be able to get only 5 percent of their protein from animal products.

According to annual polls by the Gallup organization, only about 5 percent of Americans follow a vegetarian diet. Worldwide an estimated 5 to 15 percent of people are vegetarians. As the number of vegetarians remains steady, meat consumption has doubled since the mid-1990s. According to the United Nations Food and Agriculture Organization, that number is expected to double again by 2050 given the economic expansion in China, India, and elsewhere that allows more people to afford beef.

MEAT, SHMEAT

Microsoft founder and philanthropist Bill Gates believes people need to develop alternatives to meat. As he wrote in his blog *The Gates Notes*, "Put simply, there's no way to produce enough meat for 9 billion people. . . . [We need to] work on creating alternatives to meat and eggs that are just as healthful, are produced more sustainably, and taste great."

Gates described two companies, Beyond Meat and Hampton Creek Foods, that have been working to develop plant-based foods that taste like eggs and chicken. Food scientists at the companies turn soybeans, spices, and other plant-based foods into protein-rich meat substitutes that closely resemble the taste and texture of the real thing. These products can be produced using a fraction of the water needed to raise livestock and can be manufactured on a scale large enough to feed a growing population.

Those who don't want to switch to a meat substitute might someday eat animal flesh grown in a laboratory. Lab meat—known as in vitro meat, cultured meat, or shmeat—was first produced by Dutch scientists in 2012. The shmeat beef burger is made from the muscle cells of cows, treated with a protein that promotes tissue growth.

Shmeat remains an expensive novelty, but scientists are working to perfect the method and bring down prices. Some researchers say that with the proper growing conditions, 50,000 tons (45,360 metric tons) of shmeat could be produced in two months from only ten muscle cells. The animal rights organization PETA (People for the Ethical Treatment of Animals) calls shmeat "meat without slaughter," since animals are not killed to produce it. In 2012 the organization offered $1 million to anyone who could produce commercially viable lab-grown chicken meat by 2016. More than thirty research labs worldwide have entered the competition to provide shmeat to the meat-hungry public.

MEATLESS MONDAYS

While scientists and food corporations work on developing alternatives to slaughtering animals for meat, the Meatless Monday organization, based in Baltimore, Maryland, educates people on the health and environmental benefits of giving up meat altogether—or at least for one day a week. Launched with the Johns Hopkins Bloomberg School of Public Health in 2003, Meatless Monday is active in thirty-four countries. The American Meat Institute has estimated that almost 20 percent of US households are participating in Meatless Monday.

Programs such as Meatless Monday are among dozens worldwide aimed at reducing agricultural water use and promoting good health. From the farm field to the dinner table, people are learning that wasting water is no longer an option. In the coming years, water and food costs are expected to rise worldwide due to increased demand in the face of shrinking resources. Farmers and the general public will have to shift gears.

Chapter 3

SUPPLY AND DEMAND

Compared to people in other nations, Americans pay very little for water. But as aquifers and reservoirs dry up, water prices are likely to rise in the United States.

Many people in the United States think of water as an affordable resource. In 2014 the typical price of tap water was less than one-tenth of a cent per gallon (3.7 liters) in cities such as Chicago, Illinois, and even in drought-stricken Phoenix, Arizona. The country's most expensive tap water, about 2 cents per gallon, is in Atlanta, Georgia. While water companies across the nation are raising rates around 5 percent a year, tap water remains an amazing bargain. Because of the low cost, many Americans tend to use water freely. On average, Americans use about 100 gallons (380 liters) of water every day per person, four times the amount used in China.

Of the water that comes out of the typical American's tap, very little is used for drinking, however. On average, a typical US adult drinks only about 0.5 gallon (2 liters) of water from the tap a day. The rest of the tap water—up to 95 percent—goes toward flushing toilets, bathing, laundry, washing dishes, and watering lawns.

CREAKY AND LEAKY

Around the world, city water systems are a source of great waste. In many poor nations, dams, sewers, and water mains (large pipes) are poorly maintained. According to Matthew Durnin, science director at The Nature Conservancy, an environmental protection organization,

"There's a lot of waste in urban environments, in the transfer of water in the pipes. There's literally hundreds of millions of miles of pipe laid around the world that are leaking and wasting water."

The United States has more than 170,000 municipal water systems, which supply water to more than 264 million people. These systems contain a total of 1 million miles (1.6 million km) of water mains—enough to stretch to the moon and back two times. But many of the systems were first built in the 1800s. Despite routine maintenance, the old pipes are crumbling and sometimes break. When a water main breaks, water service is disrupted. Water gushes from pipes, flooding streets and damaging buildings. According to the American Society of Civil Engineers (ASCE), an organization that designs, constructs, and studies water systems and other infrastructure, an estimated 240,000 water mains break each year in the United States. Together, these breaks waste billions of gallons of precious water annually.

The ASCE says that old drinking water delivery systems need to be replaced—but the cost will be high. The organization observes that "at the dawn of the 21st century, much of our drinking water infrastructure is nearing the end of its useful life. . . . Assuming every pipe would need to be replaced, the cost over the coming decades could reach more than $1 trillion."

The crumbling, leaking New York City water delivery system is a good example of how water is wasted on a massive scale in the United States. The five boroughs of New York City are home to nearly 9 million people. The city's water delivery system is the largest and most complex in the United States. While it performs a vital service, most of the system's pipes, like those in most American cities, are underground and largely invisible to the people who depend on them.

The New York system delivers 1.3 billion gallons (4.9 billion liters) of water to New Yorkers every day. The water comes to the city through three aqueducts—extensive aboveground and underground

FAST FACT

A person who leaves the tap running while brushing his or her teeth wastes 3,000 gallons (11,356 liters) of water per year.

channels connected to streams, lakes, and reservoirs (artificial lakes) outside the city. Altogether, the New York City water system contains 6,500 miles (10,460 km) of aqueducts that carry water under the city and pipes that carry water to individual buildings. Some of this infrastructure is located as deep as 1,000 feet (305 m) underground.

Some New York City water pipes are more than 150 years old, installed with the first city water systems in the mid-1800s. These pipes, made of clay and cast iron, are disintegrating and leaky. The Delaware Aqueduct is full of leaky pipes. Constructed between 1937 and 1945, the aqueduct provides about 65 percent of the city's daily water needs. Drawing from four reservoirs, the 84-mile (135 km) aqueduct has also been leaking an estimated 35 million gallons (132 million liters) of freshwater daily for decades—enough water every day to supply the needs of 350,000 Americans. The leaks were first discovered in the late 1980s. Because of the expense and the complicated processes required to fix leaks, city politicians waited for decades to address the problem. They finally decided to build a $1.5 billion tunnel to bypass the worst leaking sections of the aqueduct. The project, which began in 2010, is planned for completion sometime after 2021. When completed, the old sections will be sealed with concrete and abandoned.

Two tunnels currently carry water under New York City. Tunnel No. 1 was completed in 1917, while Tunnel No. 2 was put online in 1936. Both have been in continuous service since the day they opened, and both are decrepit and leaking millions of gallons of water a day. Engineers fear that one or both of the tunnels might cave in. If such a disaster were to occur, New York City would face serious water

A water main broke, flooding parts of downtown Columbus, Ohio, in January 2013. Temperatures then were below zero, and the water immediately froze, complicating repairs. Here workers fix the water main, located several feet below city streets.

shortages for two or three years. According to former New York City mayor Michael Bloomberg, "The city could be brought to its knees if one of the aqueducts collapses."

In 1970 construction began on a third tunnel, Tunnel No. 3, one of the biggest public works projects on Earth. Because of its sheer size, the tunnel will take decades to build. It is due for completion in 2020. Tunnel No. 3 is 600 feet (183 m) belowground (a depth equal to the height of a sixty-story skyscraper). It will be 60 miles (97 km) long when finished and is expected to cost more than $6 billion in total. Once Tunnel No. 3 is finished, the city can shut down the other two tunnels for major repairs.

AFRICA'S WATER-SCARCE ENVIRONMENT

While water infrastructure in the United States has problems, most Americans still receive a steady supply of safe, clean drinking water. This is not the situation in Africa and in many other parts of the world. In much of Africa, clean water is an expensive and increasingly rare commodity. About one-third of Africa's 1 billion people live in what experts call a water-scarce environment, in which they get by with only about 5 gallons (20 liters) of water per person per day. According to the United Nations, a human being needs about 13 gallons (50 liters) of water per day to drink, prepare meals, and maintain personal hygiene. Five gallons a day do not meet these basic needs.

Achim Steiner, executive director of the United Nations Environment Programme (UNEP), explains that Africa's water problems stem more from economic conditions than from environmental factors. He writes, "Africa is not water scarce. The rainfall contribution is more than adequate to meet the needs of the current population several times over. . . . The water crisis in Africa is more of an economic problem from lack of investment, and not a matter of physical scarcity."

The water infrastructure in most African cities is old, leaky, and poorly maintained. In addition, water systems commonly serve only wealthy city neighborhoods. They do not provide water to the slum areas that are home to the vast majority of African city dwellers. Most

A woman in Sierra Leone pumps water from a well built by the United Nations. Many African communities have no water delivery systems, so women typically walk many miles to gather water from wells, lakes, or rivers.

rural areas of Africa also lack water and sewer lines. Without water delivery systems, many Africans either collect water from polluted streams and lakes or buy their water from public standpipes. These outdoor pipes, with taps for dispensing water, are often filthy and poorly maintained.

In Africa women and teen girls have the traditional responsibility for collecting water. They walk long distances and wait in long lines to fill up their water jugs from waterways or standpipes. Global water expert Maude Barlow describes the situation in Kenya: "[It] is not uncommon for women to walk six hours a day to find water for their families." And once a water jug is filled, it can weigh as much as 40 pounds (18 kg). According to the United Nations, Africans spend a total of 40 billion working hours each year carrying water. The tedious chore leaves much of the female population little time to earn a living or attend school, keeping women trapped in poverty.

In many African cities, water theft is rampant. Desperate for water, people steal it from supply pipes in neighborhoods that do have water service. Another option is to buy water from neighbors who are connected to the water supply. Those who sell the water to their poor neighbors often hike up the price greatly, taking advantage of the dire need for water. Economist Michel Camdessus explains it this way:

> Poor households in the slums of cities such as Lagos [Nigeria] or Nairobi [Kenya] are paying more for their water than the rich, who are served by water utilities [companies]. Unequal access means that poorer urban residents pay as much as 50 times more per liter of water [buying from resellers] than their richer neighbors. In the Nairobi slum of Kibera, for example, some of the world's poorest people buy some of its most expensive water.

ROOFTOP GARDENS

In 2007 New York City began a program to encourage residents to capture rainwater and put it to good use. City leaders offered tax breaks to building owners who would install gardens on rooftops, large spaces that are underused in the crowded city of concrete and steel.

Rooftop gardens capture rainwater that would otherwise end up in gutters and sewers. In gardens, the water helps give life to grasses, flowers, fruits, and vegetables. In addition, rooftop gardens provide a thick layer of insulation, blocking the passage of heat and cold between the outdoors and indoors. This process keeps buildings cooler in the summer and warmer in the winter, reducing energy use.

New York City has an estimated 1 billion square feet (93 million sq. m) of roof space that could be converted from black tar to green gardens. Since the launch of the rooftop program, large rooftop gardens have been installed all over the city. The Bronx County Courthouse and the Brooklyn Ikea store have created rooftop gardens. The green roof atop the US Postal Service's Morgan Processing and Distribution Center sits seven stories above the streets of Manhattan. At nearly 2.5 acres (1 hectare), it is the largest rooftop garden in New York City and one of the largest in the country.

People have planted a garden and built a greenhouse on the top of this apartment building in New York City. Rainfall waters the garden instead of flowing into gutters and then into storm sewers.

RAINWATER CATCHERS

To meet their water needs, many Africans use one of the simplest, oldest, and cheapest water delivery systems in the world: rain catchment, or rain harvesting. In villages, people set up a series of interconnected gutters on public buildings such as medical clinics and schools. The water from the linked gutters flows to large, concrete tanks capable of holding around 25,000 gallons (94,635 liters) each. Community members collect water from the tanks whenever they need it.

Rainwater harvesting systems are inexpensive to construct and easy to maintain. They are especially useful in regions where rains are seasonal, since people can collect water during the rainy season and then use it throughout the dry season.

Catchment systems like the one in Nzatani, Kenya, have dramatically improved lives. In 2008 unskilled volunteers in the community collected the sand, gravel, and water to make cement to build the system's storage tank. Since its construction, the Nzatani rain harvester—which cost only $6,000 to build—has provided a steady water supply to six hundred people. Before it was built, local girls and women had to walk about 2 miles (3.2 km) to collect buckets of water from a stream.

PLANNING FOR GROWTH

Africa's population is expected to grow by 200 million by the year 2050. Many of these people will live in cities, whose populations are expected to double—to almost 654 million people—by the year 2035. This population growth will put a severe strain on nations that are already struggling to meet basic water and sanitation needs.

Africa's economic growth is already putting additional strains on the continent's water. International corporations based in Europe, the United States, Latin America, and elsewhere have started looking to Africa to start new operations, and these businesses all require water. With more people and growing industries, Africa also needs to generate more electricity, and this too requires vast amounts of water. Together, these pressures will quadruple the demand for water in Africa by the year 2040.

Where will Africa get this water? Experts point out that the continent receives enough rain to fulfill the water needs of 9 billion people, or nine times the African population. But getting this water to where it's needed will take careful planning. Many water experts say that the key to success is creating decentralized systems that are built to serve population clusters. A cluster might be a few homes or a slum with fifty thousand people. By building cluster systems that are close to the communities they serve, African communities can avoid

WATER FROM THE SEA

In coastal areas, people are turning seawater into freshwater for human consumption. The process is called desalination (*desalinate* means "to remove salt"), and communities in India, China, Africa, the Mideast, and the United States are turning to the technology to meet the growing demand for freshwater.

Basic desalination has been around for thousands of years. The process involves boiling seawater and capturing the steam. When the steam cools, it returns to its liquid state—without the salt. But boiling enough water for the needs of a large population requires expensive equipment and a great deal of energy. Most desalination plants run on electricity (generated by burning coal) or on natural gas. These fuel sources add to climate change and to the overall cost of water.

Reverse osmosis is another expensive desalination process. This process involves forcing seawater through a filter-like membrane under extremely high pressure. The salt stays on one side of the membrane while freshwater emerges on the other side. India, with oceans on three coasts, is investing heavily in reverse osmosis desalination. The Indian government plans to build five hundred facilities to process seawater by 2017. Saudi Arabia, another nation with long stretches of coastline, has twenty-eight desalination plants of different types supplying 70 percent of the kingdom's water.

building miles of expensive aqueducts and water mains, which carry a high price tag.

Digital systems are also a key part of developing Africa's water system. They are helping spread the rainwater-harvesting technology throughout the continent. UNEP has compiled digital rainwater databases for more than a dozen African countries, including Botswana, Ethiopia, Mozambique, Rwanda, Uganda, Zambia, and Zimbabwe. The information includes maps, rainfall amounts, roof surface areas in different regions, climate variations, population needs, and other information related to rainwater harvesting.

Rainwater harvesting is a smart option for both urban and rural settings. With education and investments in gutters, tanks, and other relatively inexpensive equipment, rain catchment programs can help reverse the African water crisis.

BILLIONS OF BOTTLES

Bottled water is a fairly new product. In 1980 the average American consumed only 1.6 gallons (6 liters) of bottled water annually. Around that time, the French company Perrier began advertising on US television, and expensive bottled water became a trendy accessory. Dozens of other companies jumped into the highly profitable bottled water market in the years that followed.

By 2014 about 475 bottled water plants in the United States were producing six hundred brands of bottled water. The average American was drinking 30 gallons (114 liters) of bottled water annually. Nationwide, Americans were consuming a total of 10 billion gallons (38 billion liters) of bottled water each year, at a cost of $11.8 billion. Worldwide, people spent over $100 billion on bottled water. The United Nations estimates that if just one-sixth of that money ($15 billion) were spent building wells and water infrastructure, the number of people worldwide without access to clean water could be cut in half.

What many buyers of bottled water don't realize is that expensive bottled water is sometimes dirtier than cheap tap water. An investigation by the nonprofit Environmental Working Group showed that some bottled water contains industrial chemicals, bacteria, and other pollution.

Bottled water also creates ecological stresses. Bottling water, transporting it to stores, and keeping it cold burns fossil fuels, which give off greenhouse gases. Additionally, plastic bottles are made from petrochemicals, derived from crude oil. Every year 17 million barrels of crude oil are used to make plastic bottles. And the bottles have created a pollution nightmare. In the United States, Americans throw away around 29 billion plastic water bottles annually. Only about 13 percent of the bottles are recycled. The rest end up in landfills or are discarded as litter along roadsides or in waterways. Many eventually flow from rivers and lakes into the ocean.

THE RIGHT TO WATER

Companies that bottle water have been draining aquifers across the globe. The Swiss food company Nestlé, for instance, has purchased water rights in Brazil, South Africa, Ethiopia, Pakistan, Canada, and elsewhere. In Pakistan, a Nestlé water bottling factory draws millions of gallons of water from an aquifer near the small village of Bhati Dilwan. Since the company set up production there in 2005, the aquifer beneath the village has dropped hundreds of feet, dramatically reducing water supplies for local residents.

Nestlé has also caused controversy in the small agricultural community of Hillsburgh, Ontario. In 2000 the company set up a water bottling plant there. The Hillsburgh government guaranteed Nestlé a continual water supply, even during times of drought. The plant pays the local water company only $3.71 for every 290,590 gallons (1.1 million liters) of water it takes from the local aquifer every day. Nestlé puts this same amount of water into plastic bottles and sells it for as much as $2 million. Local environmental groups want to see Hillsburgh cancel or severely restrict Nestlé's permit to take the water. They are part of a larger global movement that argues that water is a precious resource that should be preserved for the health of aquifers, local communities, and the ecosystem—not as a source of profit for multinational corporations.

Nestlé executives feel differently. In 2005 the company's chief executive, Peter Brabeck-Letmathe, said:

> Water is of course the most important raw material we have today in the world. It's a question of whether we should privatize [move from public to private control] the normal water supply for the population. . . . [One] opinion, which I think is extreme, is represented by [organizations] who bang on about declaring water being a public right. That means as a human being you should have a right to water. That's an extreme solution. And the other view says that water is a foodstuff like any other and like any other foodstuff it should have a market value. Personally, I believe it's better to give food stuff a value so we are all aware that it has its price.

Competition for water is increasing by the day. As the value of clean water rises, fewer people will be able to afford it and access will become increasingly limited. It will take direct action by corporations, governments, and average citizens to continue to deliver clean, safe water to a thirsty world.

An iceberg calves from a glacier in the Tracy Arm-Fords Terror Wilderness in Alaska. Glaciers are melting at an alarming rate in the Arctic, leading to rising sea levels and changing weather patterns on Earth.

Chapter 4

WATER IN A CHANGING CLIMATE

According to NASA, the ten hottest years on record have all occurred since 1998. In the United States, 2012 was the hottest year since records were first kept in the 1880s. Over the course of 2012, more than 350 US locations hit their highest-ever temperatures. After analyzing the weather extremes of 2012, climate scientist Stefan Rahmstorf commented that these were "clearly not freak events. . . . With all the extremes that . . . have struck different parts of the globe, more and more people absolutely realize that climate change is here."

According to a UN panel on climate change, the United States has seen an average temperature rise of 2°F (1.1°C) since 1960. A 1- or 2-degree change in temperature is barely noticeable on human skin. But when that temperature change is applied across the entire surface of Earth, it can trigger unpredictable climate disruption. Climate scientists believe that even a 1-degree increase could create permanent drought conditions in the US Midwest, Africa, and elsewhere, and scientists predict that Earth's average air temperature might jump 3° to 4°F (1.6 to 2.2°C) by 2050.

Around the world, spring is arriving earlier and summer is lasting longer. For example, in the northeastern United States, the frost-free season in the 2010s begins an average of eleven days earlier than it did in the 1950s. Climate change has also brought extreme weather events. Some of the most powerful rainstorms, tornadoes, and hurricanes in recorded history have occurred in the early twenty-first century.

MELTING ICE CAPS

The dramatic effects of climate change are being seen in Antarctica, where six massive glaciers are melting at an alarming rate. Antarctica, the continent surrounding the South Pole, has the largest mass of ice on Earth. The ice contains 80 percent of the world's freshwater. In 2014 scientists at NASA's Jet Propulsion Laboratory tracked the movements of the glaciers using satellite measurements and computer models. They determined that the largest mass of ice, Thwaites Glacier, might disappear completely in two hundred years.

All this melting ice will not increase freshwater supplies on Earth because the ice melts directly into the oceans, where it mixes with salt water and becomes undrinkable. In addition, as the glaciers melt, ocean levels are expected to rise by up to 4 feet (1.2 m). This rise in sea level will swamp most of the state of Florida along with major cities including New York; New Orleans, Louisiana; Boston, Massachusetts; and London in the United Kingdom. The effects will also be felt in low-lying areas of Bangladesh, Indonesia, and the Marshall Islands.

Antarctica is not the only place where global warming is melting glaciers. Ice is melting rapidly in Greenland and in other parts of the Arctic too, also adding to rising sea levels. Scientists fear that by 2100, most of the world's coastal cities will either be troubled by regular flooding or will disappear beneath the oceans completely.

TOO DRY AND TOO WET

Climate change is disturbing normal precipitation patterns: normally dry places are flooding while typically wet places are experiencing drought. Between 2005 and 2009, a drought in Georgia dried up Lake Lanier, the state's main reservoir. In 2009 rainy Seattle, Washington, received no rainfall for a record-breaking thirty days. Drought and warmer winters are also shrinking the largest source of freshwater in North America. The water levels of the Great Lakes began falling in 1998 and reached historic lows in 2013.

With less rainfall globally, droughts are increasing around the world. In East Africa, for example, a catastrophic fourteen-month drought began in July 2011 and threatened the livelihood of more than 9.5 million people. Without water, crops failed and livestock died. Widespread starvation impacted Uganda, Ethiopia, Kenya, and other parts of eastern Africa. Somalia was hit particularly hard. Almost all Somalis are small-scale farmers. They lack irrigation systems and depend on seasonal rains for survival. After the rains failed in 2011 and again in 2012, an estimated 260,000 Somalis died

The drought that struck eastern Africa in 2011 dried up lakes and rivers. Crops withered, leading to widespread famine. This cow died near the border of Kenya and Somalia.

of starvation. Half of the dead were aged five or under. A study by British scientists showed that changing rainfall patterns were behind the tragedy. Senait Gebregziabher, the Somalia director for the aid group Oxfam, commented on the findings:

> Climate change is not a threat that may hurt us in the future, because it is already causing a rise [in] humanitarian needs. In the coming decades, unless urgent action is taken to slash greenhouse gas emissions, temperatures in East Africa will continue to rise and rainfall patterns will change. This will create major problems for food production and availability.

Rajiv Shah of the US Agency for International Development (USAID) added: "There's no question that hotter and drier growing conditions in sub-Saharan Africa have reduced the resiliency of these communities. Absolutely the change in climate has contributed to this problem, without question."

After two years of crop failure, the rains finally returned to Somalia. Rather than help the stricken country, however, the precipitation caused devastation. The rains, which are usually light, came in torrents. On September 27, 2012, a year's worth of rain fell on Somalia in a single night. Fields turned to mud, and rivers overflowed their banks. Waterlogged crops died, and dozens of villages were washed away.

The United States has experienced a similar pattern of intense rains following extremely dry periods. In Colorado, for example, a prolonged drought in 2012 led to the state's second-driest year on record. Then, in 2013, Colorado had its warmest spring and summer on record and the most destructive wildfires in the state's history. The wildfires wiped out thousands of acres of trees and destroyed more than twenty-five thousand structures.

SUPERSTORM SANDY

Scientists view hurricanes as giant heat engines: they transfer heat from the ocean to the atmosphere. This heat transfer creates energy in the form of hurricane-force winds and giant waves. The more heat that is pumped into the system, the stronger the energy produced.

Kevin Trenberth, a senior scientist at the US National Oceanic and Atmospheric Administration, explains that global warming has led to stronger hurricanes: "High sea surface temperatures lead to the evaporation of moisture, which provides fuel for the storm. Then it gives up the heat: that is what powers the storm. Together they provide for stronger storms."

Trenberth points to the destructive force of Superstorm Sandy to back up his findings. The hurricane formed in the Caribbean Sea and moved onshore near Atlantic City, New Jersey, on October 29, 2012. The sea temperatures along the East Coast were more than 5°F (3°C) above average when Sandy approached. About 1°F (0.6°C) of this heat was due to climate change. According to Trenberth, this single degree of warmth "boosted rainfall by as much as 5% to 10% over what it would have been 40 years ago."

Sandy was the largest Atlantic hurricane on record, spanning more than 1,100 miles (1,800 km). The hurricane destroyed towns along the New Jersey shore. Its floodwaters swamped streets and subway tunnels in New York City. At least 266 people were killed in seven counties, and damages in the United States were more than $65 billion.

On September 12, 2013, Colorado went from drought to deluge. The state was swamped with a year's worth of rain in about twenty-four hours. The rains caused the type of flooding expected only once every thousand years. Flooding along the eastern side of the Rocky Mountains destroyed more than fifteen hundred homes and thirty highway bridges and caused more than $1 billion in damage. The city of Boulder received 17 inches (43 cm) of rain in a single day during what is typically the city's driest month.

After the rains ended, Coloradans discovered that waste treatment plants had been flooded and that sewer lines had been torn out by raging waters. Millions of gallons of raw sewage had flowed into rivers. In the town of Lyons, *E. coli* bacteria were discovered in drinking water. If ingested, *E. coli* can cause stomach cramps, vomiting, diarrhea, and even death. The flooding also affected around eighteen hundred oil and gas drilling sites in northwestern Colorado. The waters damaged storage tanks and other equipment, releasing fuel, heavy metals, and fracking fluids into local water supplies.

THE WATER CYCLE

Scientists blame the excessive droughts and floods on changes in Earth's hydrologic, or water, cycle. The hydrologic cycle is the process in which water evaporates into the air and falls as rain or snow. The oceans are the largest contributor to the water cycle. When sunlight hits seawater, the water evaporates, or turns into gaseous water vapor. The vapor rises into the atmosphere and forms clouds, which release the water as rain and snow. NASA's Earth Observatory website explains that "one expected effect of climate change will be an increase in precipitation intensity: a larger proportion of rain will fall in a shorter amount of time than it has historically."

The water cycle of the Great Lakes has been affected by higher temperatures. For instance, the portion of Lake Superior that is typically covered in winter ice has shrunk 80 percent since the early 1970s. Less ice on the lake means that more water is evaporating. Lake researcher Jay Austin explains, "When you have more open water, you have more surface to evaporate off of. You don't evaporate an enormous amount of water when you have good ice cover. Whereas when you take that ice cover away, you have a much greater potential for evaporation." Greater amounts of water vapor in the air have led to higher rain- and snowfall in areas around the lakes. The greater rates of evaporation have also contributed to dropping water levels in the Great Lakes, placing a significant strain on that valuable resource of freshwater.

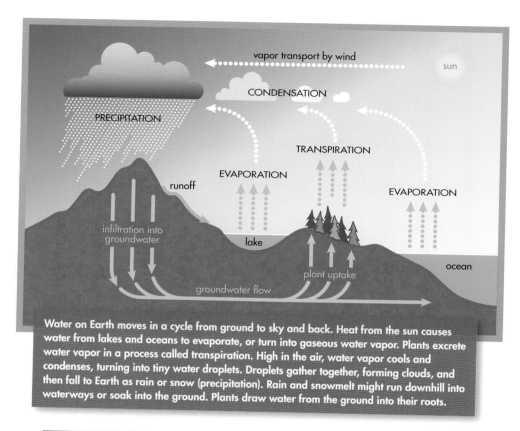

Water on Earth moves in a cycle from ground to sky and back. Heat from the sun causes water from lakes and oceans to evaporate, or turn into gaseous water vapor. Plants excrete water vapor in a process called transpiration. High in the air, water vapor cools and condenses, turning into tiny water droplets. Droplets gather together, forming clouds, and then fall to Earth as rain or snow (precipitation). Rain and snowmelt might run downhill into waterways or soak into the ground. Plants draw water from the ground into their roots.

SHRINKING SNOWPACK

Due to higher atmospheric temperatures, more precipitation is falling as rain rather than snow. This trend is affecting the snowpack, the buildup of snow that falls in mountains. Traditionally the snowpack acts as a natural water-storage facility. It grows during winter snowstorms and stores water in frozen form. In early spring, the snow slowly begins to melt, releasing freshwater into streams and rivers. As summer follows, the snowpack melts faster, supplying water to farmers and communities during the dry months.

For thousands of years, snowpack runoff has been a vital source of drinking water and irrigation for people throughout the world. Snowpack in the Rocky Mountains, for example, feeds the Colorado River and the smaller rivers and streams that flow into it. These rivers supply water to 70 million people in Phoenix; San Diego, California; Las Vegas, Nevada; and other cities of the American Southwest. The Colorado River waters also irrigate farms in California.

Because of warming temperatures, less snow is accumulating in the winter in mountainous regions of the American Southwest as well as in other parts of the world. And the snow is melting faster due to warmer, rainier springs. As a result, the snowpack is flowing away in spring too quickly to be absorbed into the soil and to be used by farmers. Faster melting also means reservoirs are overwhelmed in the spring, with more water coming in than reservoirs can hold and with the excess running off onto surrounding lands. This situation is particularly troublesome in regions such as the arid American Southwest, where water resources are naturally limited yet populations and demand for water are growing steadily. As Stanford University climate change researcher Noah Diffenbaugh explains it:

> If we look at the systems that humans currently have in place for managing water resources, we see that much of the Northern Hemisphere is dependent on snowpack for water storage. . . . [Global] warming will put increasing pressure on both flood control in the cold season and water availability in the dry season, and . . . these changes are likely to occur in some of the most densely populated and water-stressed areas of the planet.

In some cold, mountainous places of the world, the snowpack accumulates faster than it melts. Over the course of hundreds of years, the snow packs down into dense ice formations called glaciers. The Tibetan Plateau in the Himalayan range has more than fifteen hundred glaciers. This plateau stretches through portions of India, Pakistan, Afghanistan, China, Bhutan, and Nepal.

The vast Himalayan glaciers are known as the Water Towers of Asia. They contain the world's largest freshwater supply outside the polar ice caps. Waters from melting Himalayan glaciers feed huge Asian rivers, including the Ganges, the Brahmaputra, the Yangtze, the Indus, and the Mekong. Ancient civilizations grew and thrived along the shores of these rivers for thousands of years. In the twenty-first century, 1.3 billion people—about one-sixth of the world's population—depend on the Water Towers of Asia for survival.

But in 2005, researchers discovered that two-thirds of the Himalayan glaciers were melting at an alarming rate due to climate change. This melting will exacerbate water shortages in surrounding nations. As environmental journalist Steven Solomon writes, "In the next decade, they're going to need every drop they can get. Heavily populated nations from Pakistan and India to China and Cambodia face mounting, grave threats from a widespread crisis of freshwater scarcity."

Since 2010 China has moved to take control of a larger share of the water in the Tibetan Plateau. China plans to build more than 200 miles (322 km) of canals to divert melting Himalayan glacier water to the parched Yellow River.

Glaciers in the Himalayan range are melting more quickly than in the past. The people of Asia rely on the slow and steady meltwater from Himalayan glaciers to flow into lakes and rivers. With less snowfall and quickly melting glaciers, this supply might dry up.

CHINA DRIES UP

The world's most populous country, China has more than 1.3 billion people—roughly 20 percent of Earth's population. However, China has only about 7 percent of the planet's freshwater, and supplies have decreased dramatically in the past few decades due to drought and overuse.

In the 1950s, China had about fifty thousand medium to large rivers. By 2013 that number was down to twenty-three thousand. In the Chifeng region of northeastern China, farm fields have turned to deserts as rivers and aquifers have dried up. Huge cracks up to 33 feet (10 m) deep have opened up in the dry soil.

About two-thirds of China's 660 cities have less water than they need, and about 110 cities face severe shortages. In addition, water levels are declining in China's two largest rivers, the Yellow and the Yangtze. Since the 1970s, the aquifer that supplies water to Beijing, China's capital city, has dropped nearly 1,000 feet (305 m). By 2014 Beijing was suffering an acute water shortage.

WATER WARS

US novelist Mark Twain once remarked, "Whiskey's for drinking, water's for fighting." Twain was talking about nineteenth-century feuds between western US cattle ranchers and farmers, who went to blows over water rights in the newly expanding western frontier of the United States. Battles over the glacial water of the Tibetan Plateau could have much more serious consequences. As Ismail Serageldin, environmental expert for the World Bank, states, "The wars of the next century will be over water."

So far, nations are arguing but have not come to blows over water rights. However, the London-based peace organization International Alert warned in 2008 that dozens of countries might experience violent conflict over freshwater by 2025. With changing weather patterns and growing populations, it will take an unprecedented level of cooperation between and among nations to find solutions to the problem of dwindling freshwater resources in the twenty-first century.

CLIMATE ACTION PLANS

Climate change is inextricably linked with the global water crisis, and in February 2014, US secretary of state John Kerry said that climate change was one of the most serious problems facing the planet. Kerry called on all nations to respond to the problem. He referred to climate change as "the greatest challenge of our generation."

The United States has made efforts to lower carbon dioxide emissions. For instance, in June 2014 President Barack Obama proposed new EPA regulations to cut carbon pollution from power plants, with a goal of reducing emissions to 30 percent of 2005 levels by 2030. If enacted, the regulations would close hundreds of coal-fired power plants, which in 2012 produced 40 percent of all US carbon emissions, and would promote the use of solar, wind, and other alternative forms of energy.

ECOLOGICAL MIGRANTS

Across the globe, people have been forced to leave their homes because of drought and other climate extremes. The dusty county of Minqin in northern China suffers from severe water shortages due to drought. There, the government-controlled water company turns on the taps for only one hour every five days. Water shortages have forced nearly ten thousand people to leave the area. The displaced people are referred to in China as *shengtai yimin*, or "ecological migrants."

During the 2012 drought, millions of Somalis also became ecological migrants, forced to move to temporary camps in Ethiopia, Kenya, and elsewhere because of catastrophic drought. Other people might become ecological migrants because of rising sea levels caused by climate change. As sea levels rise, the Pacific island nation of Kiribati is going under water. Scientists say that the nation's thirty-two islands might all be submerged by the 2060s. To care for its one hundred thousand residents, the Kiribati government has purchased land on the neighboring island nation of Fiji, with plans to relocate Kiribati citizens there if necessary.

A power plant in Hebei Province in China burns coal to create electricity. Burning coal and other fossil fuels releases massive amounts of climate-changing carbon dioxide into the atmosphere. China, the United States, and other nations hope to reduce carbon emissions by switching from fossil fuels to renewable energy sources.

In 2012 China produced the largest amount of carbon emissions of any nation on Earth, about 27 percent of the world's total. (The United States produced the second-largest amount.) To reduce its emissions, in 2013 China invested $294 billion in renewable energy, such as solar and wind power. By 2035 China plans to generate more electricity from renewables than the United States, Europe, and Japan combined.

Despite these positive steps, experts say that renewables will produce only around 14 percent of the world's energy by 2035. Coal and oil are still cheap and abundant and remain central to the world economy. As Secretary Kerry made plain, "The energy market is a $6 trillion market with, today, 6 billion users, and it's going to grow to maybe 9 billion users over the course of the next 20, 30, 40 years."

In the United States, the multitrillion-dollar coal, oil, and gas industries use some of their profits to influence politicians and to fight against proposed EPA regulations concerning carbon pollution. They argue that reducing carbon emissions will involve complying with costly government regulations and investing in expensive new equipment. They say that these costs will hurt their businesses, slow the US economy, and cause people to lose jobs. Some energy companies and their allies even argue that human activities are not causing climate change, despite consensus on the issue by 97 percent of the world's climate scientists.

Even if politics were removed from the equation, climate change will continue into the foreseeable future. That's because reducing carbon emissions significantly will be a daunting task. For instance, to achieve a 50 percent reduction in carbon emissions by 2060, all cars on the road would need to run on half the amount of gas they currently use, one million wind turbines would have to go online, the number of nuclear power plants (which produce electricity but also produce deadly radioactive waste) would need to double, and every coal power plant would have to be shuttered. Is this goal possible?

GETTING ON NATURE'S SIDE

The large oceans that make Earth a brilliant blue marble are unique. Water nurtured the first life on Earth three billion years ago, and creatures have depended on freshwater from the primeval age to the digital era. But global threats to freshwater are unprecedented in human history. As Earth's population continues to grow, life-giving waters are overused, polluted, and wasted. And perils posed by climate change overshadow the best human efforts. Never before have so many people depended on such a fragile and finite resource.

Humanity must work with the natural forces of Earth to find cleaner ways to power the world. California governor Jerry Brown summed up the situation when he declared a statewide drought emergency in January 2014: "This is not a [political] adversary. This is Mother Nature. We have to get on nature's side and not abuse the resources that we have."

SOURCE NOTES

4   Robert Kandel, *Water from Heaven* (New York: Columbia University Press, 2003), 2.

9   Ohio Historical Society, "Cuyahoga River Fire," *Teaching Cleveland*, 2013, accessed December 23, 2013, http://www.teachingcleveland.org/index.php?option=com _content&view=article&id=335:cuyahoga-river-fire&catid=167:cuyahoga-river -fire&Itemid=178.

10 "Clean Water Act's Essential Role in Restoring the Great Lakes," *EcoWatch*, October 18, 2012, http://ecowatch.com/2012/10/18/clean-water-act-turns-40.

17 "Pollutant," EPA, December 13, 2011, http://www.epa.gov/region6/6en/w/pollutant .htm.

18 Nadya Ivanova, "Toxic Water: Across Much of China, Huge Harvests Irrigated with Industrial and Agricultural Runoff," *Circle of Blue*, January 16, 2013, http://www .circleofblue.org/waternews/2013/world/toxic-water-across-much-of-china-huge -harvests-irrigated-with-industrial-and-agricultural-runoff.

18 Gu Yongqiang, "In China, Water You Wouldn't Dare Swim In, Let Alone Drink," *Time*, March 6, 2013, http://world.time.com/2013/03/06/in-china-water-you-wouldnt-dare -swim-in-let-alone-drink.

19 Ibid.

22 Lester R. Brown, "The Real Threat to Our Future Is Peak Water," *Guardian* (London), July 6, 2013, http://www.theguardian.com/global-development/2013/jul/06/water -supplies-shrinking-threat-to-food.

25 Jon Miller, "Facing Water Shortages, Indian Farmers Dig In," *Marketplace*, May 7, 2012, http://www.marketplace.org/topics/sustainability/food-9-billion/facing-water-shortages -indian-farmers-dig.

25 Ibid.

26 Anduin Kirkbride McElroy, "The Future of the Ogallala Aquifer," *Ethanol Producer*, January 1, 2008, http://www.ethanolproducer.com/articles/3570/the-future-of-the -ogallala-aquifer.

27–28 Bill Gates, "The Future of Food," *Gates Notes*, 2014, accessed May 12, 2014, http://www .gatesnotes.com/About-Bill-Gates/Future-of-Food.

31 Jaime A. FlorCruz, "On Xi's To-Do List: Fix China's Drinking Problem," *CNN*, November 23, 2012, http://www.cnn.com/2012/11/23/world/asia/chinas-drinking -problem.

31 "Drinking Water," American Society of Civil Engineers, 2014, accessed January 3, 2014, http://www.infrastructurereportcard.org/a/#p/drinking-water/overview.

33 Alex Prud'Homme, *The Ripple Effect* (New York: Scribner, 2011), 120.

34 "Rainwater Harvesting Could End Much of Africa's Water Shortage, UN Reports," *UN News Centre*, November 13, 2006, http://www.un.org/apps/news/story.asp?NewsID=205 81&Cr=unep&Cr1=water.

35   Irene Salina, ed., *Written in Water* (Washington, DC: National Geographic Society, 2010), 77.

35   Michel Camdessus, "How to Beat Africa's Water Crises," *CNN World*, August 23, 2012, http://globalpublicsquare.blogs.cnn.com/2012/08/23/how-to-beat-africas-water-crisis.

41   Anthony Gucciardi, "Nestle CEO: Water Is Not a Human Right, Should Be Privatized," *Natural Society*, April 23, 2013, http://naturalsociety.com/nestle-ceo-water -not-human-right-should-be-privatized.

42   Seth Borenstein, "2012 Extreme Weather Sets Records, Fits Climate Change Forecasts," *Huffington Post*, December 12, 2012, http://www.huffingtonpost .com/2012/12/21/2012-extreme-weather-climate-change_n_2348079.html.

45   Jason Straziuso, "Somalia Famine Killed 260,000, Report Estimates," *Huffington Post*, March, 29, 2013, http://www.huffingtonpost.com/2013/04/29/somalia-famine -2011_n_3177741.html.

45   Joshua Hersh, "East Africa Famine Threatens Regional Stability, USAID Chief Says," *Huffington Post*, July 13, 2011, http://www.huffingtonpost.com/2011/07/13/famine-in -africa-usaid_n_897644.

46   John McQuaid, "Hurricanes and Climate Change," *NOVA*, November 15, 2012, http:// www.pbs.org/wgbh/nova/earth/hurricanes-climate.html.

46   Ibid.

47   Paul Przyborski, "The Water Cycle and Climate Change," *Earth Observatory*, 2011, accessed December 15, 2013, http://earthobservatory.nasa.gov/Features/Water/page3 .php.

47   Dan Kraker, "Great Lakes Water Levels Reaching Historic Lows," *MPR News*, April 23, 2013, http://www.mprnews.org/story/2013/04/23/environment/great-lakes-water -levels-reaching-record-lows.

49   Rob Jordan, "Stanford Study: Climate Change Threatens Freshwater Source for Billions," *Stanford Report*, November 11, 2012, http://news.stanford.edu/news/2012 /november/future-snowpack-decline-111112.html.

50   Steve Solomon, "The Struggle for Asia's Water Begins," *Forbes*, September 9, 2010, http://www.forbes.com/2010/09/09/water-china-tibet-2020-opinions-contributors -steven-solomon.html.

51   Prud'Homme, *Ripple Effect*, 198.

51   Ibid.

52   John Kerry, "Remarks on Climate Change," US Department of State, February 16, 2014, http://www.state.gov/secretary/remarks/2014/02/221704.

53   Ibid.

54   Bettina Boxall and Anthony York, "Brown Declares Drought," *Los Angeles Times*, January 18, 2014, A1.

GLOSSARY

aqueduct: any system of pipes, channels, tunnels, and other structures used to convey water from a source to a populated area

aquifer: naturally occurring layers of freshwater found underground. The Ogallala is the largest known aquifer on Earth.

biofuel: fuel produced from plants, such as corn, to power vehicles

desalination: removing salt and other minerals from seawater to produce freshwater for human consumption

drought: an extended period of below-average rainfall, generally less than 10 inches (25 cm) annually

evaporation: the process in which liquid turns into gas. Evaporation is caused by heat.

glacier: a large mass of slow-moving ice, formed by packed snow that has built up over many years, usually centuries

hydraulic fracturing: breaking apart underground layers of rock to release natural gas and oil by injecting high-pressure fluids underground; also called fracking

hydrologic cycle: the process in which water evaporates into the air, forms clouds, and falls back to Earth as rain or snow

irrigation: the watering of land, typically for agricultural use, through devices such as canals, pipes, sprinklers, and reservoirs

rain catchment: a method of using receptacles and other systems to catch rainwater; also called rainwater harvesting

renewable energy: energy that comes from sources that are naturally replenished. Examples include sunlight, wind power, hydropower, and geothermal power (power from the heat of Earth).

reservoir: an artificial lake built for holding large amounts of water

snowpack: layers of snow that accumulate in mountain regions during cold weather. In warm weather, melting water from the snowpack flows into streams and rivers.

SELECTED BIBLIOGRAPHY

Borenstein, Seth. "2012 Extreme Weather Sets Records, Fits Climate Change Forecasts." *Huffington Post*, December 12, 2012. http://www.huffingtonpost.com/2012/12/21/2012 -extreme-weather-climate-change_n_2348079.html.

Boxall, Bettina, and Anthony York. "Brown Declares Drought." *Los Angeles Times*, January 18, 2014.

Brown, Lester R. "The Real Threat to Our Future Is Peak Water." *Guardian* (London), July 6, 2013. http://www.theguardian.com/global-development/2013/jul/06/water-supplies-shrinking -threat-to-food.

Camdessus, Michel. "How to Beat Africa's Water Crises." *CNN World*, August 23, 2012. http:// globalpublicsquare.blogs.cnn.com/2012/08/23/how-to-beat-africas-water-crisis.

"Clean Water Act's Essential Role in Restoring the Great Lakes." *EcoWatch*, October 18, 2012. http://ecowatch.com/2012/10/18/clean-water-act-turns-40.

Cope, Gord. "Pure Water, Semiconductors and the Recession." *Global Water Intelligence*, October 2009. Accessed May 12, 2014. http://www.globalwaterintel.com/archive/10/10/market -insight/pure-water-semiconductors-and-the-recession.html.

"Devoted to Fighting Fracking." *Politico*, July 7, 2013. http://www.politico.com/story/2013/07 /fighting-fracking-rapp-scroggins-93781.html.

"Drinking Water." American Society of Civil Engineers. 2014. Accessed January 3, 2014. http:// www.infrastructurereportcard.org/a/#p/drinking-water/overview.

Fears, Darryl. "Bay's Intersex Fish Mystery Remains Unsolved." *Washington Post*, March 17, 2013. http://www.washingtonpost.com/national/health-science/bays-intersex-fish-mystery -remains-unsolved/2013/03/17/7f368734-8746-11e2-9d71-f0feafdd1394_story.html.

FlorCruz, Jaime A. "On Xi's To-Do List: Fix China's Drinking Problem." *CNN*, November 23, 2012. http://www.cnn.com/2012/11/23/world/asia/chinas-drinking-problem.

Ganzel, Bill. "Center Pivots Take Over." *Wessels Living History Farm*. 2006. Accessed May 12, 2014. http://www.livinghistoryfarm.org/farminginthe50s/water_03.html.

Gates, Bill. "The Future of Food." *Gates Notes*. 2014. Accessed May 12, 2014. http://www .gatesnotes.com/About-Bill-Gates/Future-of-Food.

Gucciardi, Anthony. "Nestle CEO: Water Is Not a Human Right, Should Be Privatized." *Natural Society*, April 23, 2013. http://naturalsociety.com/nestle-ceo-water-not-human-right -should-be-privatized.

Hansen, James. "Twenty Years Later: Tipping Points Near on Global Warming." *Huffington Post*, June 23, 2008. http://www.huffingtonpost.com/dr-james-hansen/twenty-years-later -tippin_b_108766.html.

Hersh, Joshua. "East Africa Famine Threatens Regional Stability, USAID Chief Says." *Huffington Post*, July 13, 2011. http://www.huffingtonpost.com/2011/07/13/famine-in-africa -usaid_n_897644.html.

Ivanova, Nadya. "Toxic Water: Across Much of China, Huge Harvests Irrigated with Industrial and Agricultural Runoff." *Circle of Blue*, January 16, 2013. http://www.circleofblue.org /waternews/2013/world/toxic-water-across-much-of-china-huge-harvests-irrigated-with -industrial-and-agricultural-runoff.

Jordan, Rob. "Stanford Study: Climate Change Threatens Freshwater Source for Billions." *Stanford Report*, November 11, 2012. http://news.stanford.edu/news/2012/november/future -snowpack-decline-111112.html.

Kandel, Robert. *Water from Heaven*. New York: Columbia University Press, 2003.

Kerry, John. "Remarks on Climate Change." US Department of State, February 16, 2014. http://www.state.gov/secretary/remarks/2014/02/221704.htm.

Kraker, Dan. "Great Lakes Water Levels Reaching Historic Lows." *MPR News*, April 23, 2013. http://www.mprnews.org/story/2013/04/23/environment/great-lakes-water-levels-reaching -record-lows.

McElroy, Anduin Kirkbride. "The Future of the Ogallala Aquifer." *Ethanol Producer*, January 1, 2008. http://www.ethanolproducer.com/articles/3570/the-future-of-the-ogallala-aquifer.

McQuaid, John. "Hurricanes and Climate Change." *NOVA*, November 15, 2012. http://www .pbs.org/wgbh/nova/earth/hurricanes-climate.html.

Miller, Jon. "Facing Water Shortages, Indian Farmers Dig In." *Marketplace*, May 7, 2012. http:// www.marketplace.org/topics/sustainability/food-9-billion/facing-water-shortages-indian -farmers-dig.

Ohio Historical Society. "Cuyahoga River Fire." *Teaching Cleveland*. 2013. Accessed December 23, 2013. http://www.teachingcleveland.org/index.php?option=com_content&view=article&id= 335:cuyahoga-river-fire&catid=167:cuyahoga-river-fire&Itemid=178.

"Pollutant." EPA, December 13, 2011. http://www.epa.gov/region6/6en/w/pollutant.htm.

Prud'Homme, Alex. *The Ripple Effect*. New York: Scribner, 2011.

Przyborski, Paul. "The Water Cycle and Climate Change." *Earth Observatory*. 2013. Accessed December 15, 2013. http://earthobservatory.nasa.gov/Features/Water/page3.php.

"Rainwater Harvesting Could End Much of Africa's Water Shortage, UN Reports." *UN News Centre*, November 13, 2006. http://www.un.org/apps/news/story.asp?NewsID=20581&Cr=une p&Cr1=water.

Salina, Irene, ed. *Written in Water*. Washington, DC: National Geographic Society, 2010.

Solomon, Steve. "The Struggle for Asia's Water Begins." *Forbes*, September 9, 2010. http://www .forbes.com/2010/09/09/water-china-tibet-2020-opinions-contributors-steven-solomon.html.

Straziuso, Jason. "Somalia Famine Killed 260,000, Report Estimates." *Huffington Post*, March 29, 2013. http://www.huffingtonpost.com/2013/04/29/somalia-famine-2011_n_3177741.html.

Wines, Michael. "Wells Dry, Fertile Plains Turn to Dust." *New York Times*, May 19, 2013. http://www.nytimes.com/2013/05/20/us/high-plains-aquifer-dwindles-hurting-farmers .html?pagewanted=2&_r=1.

Yongqiang, Gu. "In China, Water You Wouldn't Dare Swim In, Let Alone Drink." *Time*, March 6, 2013. http://world.time.com/2013/03/06/in-china-water-you-wouldnt-dare-swim-in-let -alone-drink.

FURTHER INFORMATION

Books

DiPiazza, Francesca Davis. *Remaking the John: The Invention and Reinvention of the Toilet*. Minneapolis: Twenty-First Century Books, 2015. This book traces the history of toilets—from the ancient world's pits toilets to the high-tech toilets on the International Space Station. It discusses lack of access to sanitation systems on a global scale and the impact on water and human health.

Espejo, Roman, ed. *Adaptation and Climate Change*. Farmington Hills, MI: Greenhaven Press, 2012. This book offers articles about climate change written by scientists, researchers, and activists with varying viewpoints.

Feinstein, Stephen. *Conserving and Protecting Water*. Berkeley Heights, NJ: Enslow Publishers, 2013. Feinstein examines the world's freshwater situation, threats to drinking water, and solutions for saving and protecting this precious resource.

Gay, Kathlyn. *Food*. Minneapolis: Twenty-First Century Books, 2013. Food production requires large amounts of freshwater while factory farms produce massive amounts of wastewater. This book provides a comprehensive look at global food production and the ways it interacts with the environment, politics, and business.

Hillstrom, Kevin. *Fracking*. Farmington Hills, MI: Lucent Books, 2014. This book presents a thorough examination of hydraulic fracturing, including discussions about water use and pollution.

Kallen, Stuart. *Toxic Waste*. San Diego: ReferencePoint Press, 2010. This title examines toxic waste in the United States, cleanup efforts, and what the future holds for hazardous waste sites.

McPherson, Stephanie Sammartino. *Arctic Thaw: Climate Change and the Global Race for Energy Resources*. Minneapolis: Twenty-First Century Books, 2015. In this thoroughly researched examination of Arctic thaw, McPherson details the race to claim mineral rights in the Arctic, as global warming leads to increasing ice melt and access to previously unavailable mineral resources in the northernmost region of the world.

Parks, Peggy. *Waterborne Illnesses*. Farmington, MI: Lucent Books, 2013. Polluted water spreads numerous diseases that kill thousands of children every day. This book examines the causes of waterborne illnesses and presents solutions.

Tanaka, Shelley. *Climate Change*. Sydney, Australia: ReadHowYouWant, 2013. This book examines Earth's climate and how global warming has escalated through the burning of fossil fuels and other human activities.

Films

Chasing Ice. DVD. New York: Submarine Deluxe, 2012. This beautifully shot film follows *National Geographic* photographer James Balog as he captures images of melting polar ice, providing visual details about Earth's changing climate.

Climate Refugees. DVD. Los Angeles: LA Think Tank, 2010. This film explores how droughts, floods, and other extreme weather events are forcing millions of people to leave their homes and take refuge in foreign nations. The filmmakers interview politicians, scientists, and international AID workers to examine the existing crisis as well as how it might play out in the future.

Flow: For the Love of Water. DVD. New York: Oscilloscope Laboratories, 2008. In this documentary film, water activists and scientists explore the big-business forces behind bottled water and the move to privatize community water systems.

Gasland. DVD. Park City, UT: Sundance, 2011. This documentary film shines a light on the natural gas boom in the United States. It examines the negative effects of hydraulic fracturing, which contaminates water and air.

Gasland II. DVD. New York: HBO Documentary Films, 2013. The sequel to *Gasland*, this film shows the influence of the oil extraction industry on government and politicians.

Websites

Circle of Blue
http://www.circleofblue.org
In 2000 journalists and scientists founded this website to provide information about the world water crisis and its relationship to food, energy, and health.

EcoWatch
http://ecowatch.com
This website presents the latest news concerning a wide range of environmental topics, including water, energy, and climate change.

Food and Water Watch
http://www.foodandwaterwatch.org
This public interest organization explores issues concerning the safety and accessibility of water and food.

International Water Management Institute (IWMI)
http://www.iwmi.cgiar.org
The International Water Management Institute promotes sustainable water and land use in poor countries in Asia and Africa. The IWMI website includes articles on drought, climate change, and agriculture.

Meatless Monday
http://www.meatlessmonday.com
The Meatless Monday website features meatless recipes for every meal, articles about the Meatless Monday movement, a newsletter, and tools for starting your own Meatless Monday campaign.

Natural Resources Defense Council
http://www.nrdc.org
Hosted by one of the world's leading environmental organizations, this site provides science-based information about threats to the air, freshwater, and oceans, along with details concerning global warming, factory farming, fracking, and other ecological issues.

President Obama's Plan to Fight Climate Change
http://www.whitehouse.gov/share/climate-action-plan
This official White House website describes actions the president has taken to reduce carbon pollution and to prepare the United States for the impacts of climate change. Charts and graphs show the effects of weather extremes across the United States.

Water.org
http://www.water.org
Cofounded by actor Matt Damon, Water.org focuses on water and sanitation problems in poor countries. The website provides statistics, maps, photos, and videos that highlight the problems and also offers solutions.

INDEX

activists, 18, 24. *See also* Jin Zengmin; Singh, Rajendra

Africa: cluster systems, 38; digital systems, 39; economic growth, 37–38; economy, 34; water-scarce environment, 33–35; water theft, 35. *See also* desalination plants; drought; water delivery systems

antipollution campaigns, 18–19. *See also* Sina Weibo campaign

aquifers and overpumping, 4–5, 22–23, 40. *See also* India; Ogallala Aquifer

Bao Zhenmin, 18

beef production and contribution to water shortages, 27

bottled water: Environmental Working Group, 40; greenhouse gases, 40; Perrier, 39. *See also* Nestlé; water pollution

canal irrigation systems: ancient Egypt, 20; center-pivot irrigators, 21; drip irrigation systems, 25; the evolution of irrigation systems, 20–21

chemical spills and leaks, 10, 13, 15–17

Clean Water Act (CWA), 9, 11–12, 17. *See also* point source pollution

climate change: extreme weather, 7, 42–46; Hurricane Sandy, 46; melting glaciers, 42–43, 50. *See also* drought; flooding; global warming; hydrologic cycle

concentrated animal feeding operations (CAFOs), 12–13. *See also* factory farm industry; Great Lakes Basin; outdoor lagoons

corn and ethanol production, 26

Cuyahoga River fire, 8–9

desalination plants: basic desalination, 38; reverse osmosis, 38; Saudi Arabia, 38. *See also* India

diagram, 48

drought: in Africa, 7, 44–45; in China, 51, 52; starvation and, 7, 23, 44–45; the Syrian drought, 7; in the United States, 25, 45. *See also* climate change; India

ecological migrants, 52. *See also* sewage treatment plants

Environmental Protection Agency (EPA), 9, 12–13, 26, 52–53

factory farm industry, 12–13. *See also* concentrated animal feeding operations (CAFOs)

flooding: in East Africa, 45; in the United States, 46–47. *See also* climate change

food shortages and malnutrition, 23. *See also* India

fossil fuels, 6–7, 14, 40, 53. *See also* fracking (hydraulic fracturing); greenhouse gases

4-methylcyclohexanemethanol (MCHM) and the Charleston chemical leak, 10. *See also* Freedom Industries

fracking (hydraulic fracturing), 14–17, 47; and cancerous chemicals, 16; and flammable methane, 17. *See also* fossil fuels; fractivists; Halliburton Loophole; water pollution

fractivists, 15

Freedom Industries, 10. *See also* 4-methylcyclohexanemethanol (MCHM) and the Charleston chemical leak

Gates, Bill, 27–28

global warming, 7, 43, 46, 49. *See also* climate change; drought; fossil fuels; greenhouse gases

Great Lakes Basin, 8. *See also* concentrated animal feeding operations (CAFOs)
greenhouse gases, 7, 45

Halliburton Loophole, 17
hydrologic cycle, 47–48. *See also* climate change

India: monsoons, 23–24; water well drilling, 23. *See also* drought; food shortages and malnutrition; pond digging

Jin Zengmin, 18–19. *See also* activists; shoe factories

Kerry, John, 52–53

Nestlé, 40–41
nonpoint source pollution, 11-12

Obama, Barack, 52
Ogallala Aquifer, 5–6, 21–22, 26
outdoor lagoons, 12–13. *See also* concentrated animal feeding operations (CAFOs)
overpopulation and water demand, 5, 23, 37–38, 49, 51

point source pollution, 9
pond digging, 24–25. *See also* India; Singh, Rajendra

renewable energy, 53
rooftop gardens in New York City, 36

Safe Drinking Water Act (SDWA), 11, 15
sewage treatment plants, 9, 11–12. *See also* Environmental Protection Agency (EPA)

shoe factories, 18. *See also* Jin Zengmin
Sina Weibo campaign, 18–19
Singh, Rajendra, 24–25. *See also* activists; India; pond digging
snowpack, 48–49. *See also* climate change; flooding; global warming
vegetarianism, 27; and meat alternatives, 27–28; Meatless Monday, 28–29; PETA (People for the Ethical Treatment of Animals), 28; shmeat, 28

water: body composition, 4; bottled water, 10, 17, 39–40; as a commodity, 7, 33; contamination of, 11, 13, 16–18; demand for, 5, 29, 38, 49; on Earth, 4–5; shortages of, 22–23, 27, 50–52; types of, 4–5; uses of, 7, 18, 23–24, 27, 30, 36; water waste, 6, 30–32. *See also* Ogallala Aquifer; waterborne illnesses; water pollution; water rights
waterborne illnesses, 6
water delivery systems: Delaware Aqueduct, 32; inadequacies, 31–33; New York City water pipes, 31–33; rain catchment (rain harvesting), 37, 39. *See also* Africa
water pollution: China, 6, 17–19; polluting materials, 6–7. *See also* bottled water; fracking (hydraulic fracturing)
water rights: conflicts, 7, 51; Syrian civil war, 7; Tibetan Plateau glacial water, 50
Water Towers of Asia (Himalayan glaciers), 50. *See also* climate change; global warming

PHOTO ACKNOWLEDGMENTS

The images in this book are used with the permission of: © iStockphoto.com/ blueenayim, (cracked background); © David Madison/Moment Mobile/Getty Images, p. 4; © Chien-min Chung/In Pictures/CORBIS, p. 6; © Bettmann/CORBIS, p. 8; AP Photo/Tyler Evert, p. 10; Jim Lo Scalzo/EPA/Landov, p. 16; Alpha/Landov, p. 19; © Middle East/Alamy, p. 20; © Jim Parkin/Dreamstime.com, p. 22; © Nigel Cattlin/Alamy, p. 24; © Peter Bennett/Ambient Images Inc./Alamy, p. 30; AP Photo/ Andrew Welsh-Huggins, p. 33; © Tommy E Trenchard/Alamy, p. 34; © Picture Partners/Alamy, p. 36; © Paul Souders/CORBIS, p. 42; ©Thomas Mukoya/ CORBIS, p. 44; © Laura Westlund/Independent Picture Service, p. 48; © Jake Norton/Aurora Photos/Alamy, p. 50; © Liu Liqun/CORBIS, p. 53.

Front cover: © Yuji Kotani/Digital Vision/Getty Images (faucet); © Netfalls/ Bigstock.com (mud cracks).

Back cover: © iStockphoto.com/blueenayim (cracks).

ABOUT THE AUTHOR

Stuart A. Kallen has written more than 250 nonfiction books for children and young adults over the past twenty years. His books have covered a wide arc of human history, culture, and science, from the building of the pyramids to the music of the twenty-first century. Some of his recent titles include *The Aftermath of the Sandinista Revolution, The History of R&B and Soul Music,* and *K-Pop: Korea's Musical Explosion.* Kallen, who lives in San Diego, California, is also a singer-songwriter and guitarist.